# Illicit Core, Speculative Mantle Peeling Back the Layers of the Bitcoin Market

## Preface

Bitcoin stands as a beacon of innovation and a subject of intense speculation. This book unfolds the heart of the Bitcoin ecosystem, revealing the complexities beneath its surface. This book explores the dual nature of Bitcoin—a groundbreaking financial technology that has been celebrated for its potential yet scrutinised for the shadows that lurk within its core.

Bitcoin promised a new era of financial transactions, offering anonymity, efficiency, and decentralisation. However, as it surged in popularity and value, it became a fertile ground for speculative frenzy and a haven for illicit activities. From its speculative outer layer, where investors and enthusiasts ride the waves of its volatile price fluctuations, to its core, where obscured transactions and questionable practices dwell, Bitcoin embodies a paradoxical blend of potential and peril.

We aim to dissect these contrasting aspects of Bitcoin, providing readers with an insightful understanding of its market dynamics. The book uncovers how the allure of quick gains and the anonymity offered by Bitcoin have created a speculative mantle that attracts and distracts from its more nefarious uses. Beneath this layer of speculation lies the illicit core, a dark nexus of activities ranging from money laundering to financing illegal operations, challenging the principles upon which Bitcoin was founded.

As we peel back these layers, the book sheds light on the technical and financial features of the Bitcoin market and explores the ethical and regulatory challenges it poses. Examining the relationship between digital currency's potential for innovation and its susceptibility to misuse, we invite readers to consider the broader implications of embracing such a disruptive technology.

It is not just a story about Bitcoin; it reflects the digital age's complexities, where technological advances hold immense promise yet harbour significant risks.

# Table of Contents

# 1. Bitcoin Genesis

## 1.1. The Birth of a Digital Revolution

In the wake of the 2008 financial crisis, a profound distrust of traditional banking institutions and the global financial system began to take root among many. Against this backdrop, an individual or group under the pseudonym Satoshi Nakamoto introduced Bitcoin in a white paper titled *"Bitcoin: A Peer-to-Peer Electronic Cash System."* This seminal document proposed a novel solution to the double-spending problem without needing a trusted third party, laying the foundation for a decentralised digital currency.

Bitcoin's underlying technology, the blockchain, is a distributed ledger that records all transactions across a network of computers. This innovation not only facilitates peer-to-peer transactions without the need for intermediary financial institutions but also ensures the integrity and transparency of the entire system. The blockchain's immutable record of transactions, secured through cryptographic means, represented a paradigm shift in how digital transactions could be conducted, verified, and recorded.

For finance, technology, and cryptography experts, the introduction of Bitcoin heralded the beginning of a digital revolution with the potential to disrupt the traditional financial ecosystem. Its decentralised nature challenged the centralised models of currency control and financial oversight, proposing an alternative that was global, transparent, and resistant to censorship.

The cryptographic principles underpinning Bitcoin initially ensured security and anonymity for its users, addressing concerns about privacy in digital transactions. Moreover, the Bitcoin mining mechanism introduced a novel approach to currency issuance and distribution based on a predetermined algorithm rather than central bank policies. This aspect of Bitcoin appealed to those wary of inflationary pressures associated with traditional fiat currencies, as the total supply of Bitcoin is capped at 21 million, aiming to create scarcity and, theoretically, preserve value over time.

For experts, the significance of Bitcoin's emergence was manifold. It represented a technological innovation and a challenge to the economic and political norms governing currencies. The implications for financial markets, regulatory frameworks, and global economic systems were profound, inviting rigorous analysis and debate among academics, technologists, and policymakers.

As Bitcoin's adoption grew, so did its recognition as a groundbreaking development in the history of money. Its ability to facilitate fast, secure, and borderless transactions presented opportunities and challenges, compelling experts to reevaluate concepts of currency, value exchange, and the very structure of the global financial system. In essence, Bitcoin's birth marked the beginning of an ongoing exploration into the potential of digital currencies to reshape our understanding and interaction with money.

To the broader public, the conflation of Bitcoin and cryptocurrencies with blockchain technology is a common misconception often arising from these concepts' intertwined history and development. While Bitcoin, the first and most well-known cryptocurrency, introduced blockchain technology to the world, equating the two or using them synonymously overlooks blockchain's broader applications and potential beyond digital currencies.

## 1.2. Blockchain: the 17-year-old technology gains hype

Blockchain technology is often hailed as the backbone of cryptocurrencies like Bitcoin, and its roots are planted far deeper in the annals of digital history than many realise. Invented in 1991 by Stuart Haber and W. Scott Stornetta, two researchers who aimed to implement a system where document timestamps could not be tampered with, blockchain served as a testament to the integrity of digital documents. This innovative concept, although revolutionary, did not gain immediate prominence in the technological context.

The essence of blockchain lies in its ability to distribute information without allowing it to be copied or altered, creating an immutable ledger of transactions. This foundational principle of decentralisation and transparency was initially conceived to secure digital documents. The early application of blockchain, thus, was far from the financial speculation and transactions of today's cryptocurrencies. Instead, it aimed to create a tamper-proof, digital time-stamping service (serving a completely different function). This service would encode the hash of a document into a block, ensuring that the document's content remained unaltered over time without necessitating trust in a single authority.

Further developments in the late '90s and early 2000s, such as the introduction of the concept of a hash chain by Bayer, Haber, and Stornetta in 1992 and the development of the Merkle tree for efficient data verification processes, expanded the potential applications of blockchain. However, these innovations remained largely academic and underutilised in practical applications. It was not until 2008, with the publication of the Bitcoin whitepaper by Satoshi Nakamoto, that blockchain technology was applied to create the first decentralised digital currency.

The technical underpinnings of blockchain include a distributed ledger technology (DLT) where each block contains a timestamp and a link to the previous block, forming a chain. This design ensures the integrity and chronological order of the ledger. Security is further enhanced through cryptographic hashes, essentially digital fingerprints of the data, ensuring that any alteration of transaction data within a block is easily detectable.

Before its application in cryptocurrencies, the potential uses of blockchain were largely theoretical. The technology's capacity for ensuring data integrity without centralised oversight hinted at applications in digital notarisation, secure voting systems, and digital rights management. However, the advent of Bitcoin catapulted blockchain from an obscure technological concept to a cornerstone of digital transactions, highlighting its potential beyond securing digital documents to enabling a decentralised financial ecosystem.

Early blockchain applications lay the groundwork for many use cases beyond cryptocurrencies. Today, industries ranging from supply chain management to healthcare are exploring how blockchain's inherent properties of transparency, security, and immutability can solve longstanding challenges, demonstrating the technology's far-reaching potential beyond its cryptographic origins.

### 1.3. The Dual Appeal: Speculation and Illicit Activities

The emergence of blockchain and, subsequently, Bitcoin has prompted a new digital frontier driven by two powerful forces: speculation and illicit activities. These forces, while distinct, are deeply intertwined within the ecosystem of cryptocurrencies, presenting a dual appeal that has significantly contributed to the rapid proliferation and volatility of digital currencies.

#### 1.3.1.   Speculation: The Financial Gold Rush

On one hand, the speculative appeal of cryptocurrencies is undeniable. The decentralised nature of blockchain technology has given rise to a digital gold rush, where the value of cryptocurrencies like Bitcoin is driven by market demand rather than intrinsic value or governmental backing. It has led to great volatility, with prices subject to dramatic fluctuations based on investor sentiment, market trends, and regulatory news.

The allure of high returns has attracted many participants, from individual investors and day traders to institutional investors and hedge funds. The speculative nature of the market is amplified by the limited supply of many cryptocurrencies, particularly Bitcoin, which has a capped supply of 21 million coins. This scarcity and increasing demand have fueled speculative investment, drawing parallels with historical financial bubbles.

The speculative market for cryptocurrencies is characterised by a high degree of leverage, the use of derivatives, and the emergence of secondary markets, which allow for complex investment strategies. These financial instruments increase liquidity but also introduce additional layers of risk, highlighting the speculative fervour that defines much of the cryptocurrency market.

### 1.3.2. *Illicit Activities: The Shadow Economy*

Conversely, blockchain technology's pseudonymous and decentralised aspects have also made cryptocurrencies a preferred medium for illicit activities. The ability to transact without revealing one's identity has attracted individuals and organisations involved in activities ranging from money laundering and tax evasion to the financing of terrorism and illegal drug trade.

Cryptocurrencies offer a digital avenue for moving and hiding assets outside the purview of traditional financial institutions and regulatory frameworks. The anonymity provided by blockchain allows for the obfuscation of the origins and destinations of funds, complicating efforts by law enforcement and regulatory agencies to trace illicit transactions.

While the blockchain ledger is transparent and transactions are permanently recorded, the ability to create multiple addresses and techniques such as "mixing" or "tumbling" services further complicates the tracing of funds. These services obscure the flow of cryptocurrencies by mixing potentially identifiable or "tainted" coins with others, making it difficult to link transactions to specific individuals or entities.

The dual appeal of cryptocurrencies—rooted in the potential for speculative gains and the facilitation of illicit activities—highlights the complex nature of the digital currency landscape. While the speculative market brings liquidity and innovation, it raises concerns about market manipulation, investor protection, and financial stability. Simultaneously, using cryptocurrencies for illicit activities poses significant challenges to law enforcement, regulatory compliance, and the financial system's integrity.

Often presented as a pioneering force in the digital currency, Bitcoin diverges significantly from traditional investments like shares or bonds. This distinction primarily stems from its nature and how it generates value for its holders. Unlike traditional investment vehicles that offer returns in the form of interest or dividends, Bitcoin operates on a fundamentally different premise.

### 1.3.3.  Lack of Intrinsic Cash Flows

Shares and bonds are traditional financial instruments that provide investors with well-defined returns. Shares, or equities, represent ownership stakes in companies. Investors in shares benefit from dividends, which are portions of a company's profit paid out to shareholders. Additionally, shareholders stand to gain from appreciation in the company's stock price, which ideally reflects the company's growth and profitability over time.

Bonds, on the other hand, are debt instruments issued by corporations or governments to raise capital. Bondholders receive regular interest payments, known as coupon payments, during the bond's life, and the principal amount is repaid at maturity. Interest payments and the return on principals make bonds an investment that generates predictable income, reflecting the issuer's obligation to repay the borrowed capital with interest.

Bitcoin does not provide such cash flows. It does not pay dividends or interest because it is not a claim on a company's profits or an obligation of a borrower. The value of Bitcoin is not derived from the financial performance or profitability of an entity. Instead, it is based on supply and demand dynamics in the cryptocurrency market, which are influenced by market sentiment, adoption rates, regulatory changes, and technological advancements.

### 1.3.4.  Speculative Value and Volatility

The value of Bitcoin is largely speculative, driven by investors' expectations of future price appreciation rather than underlying economic fundamentals or cash flows. This speculative nature contributes to Bitcoin's high volatility, with prices subject to rapid fluctuations based on news, investor sentiment, and market trends. While traditional investments like stocks and bonds can also be volatile, their prices are generally anchored by underlying financial metrics and economic indicators.

### 1.3.5.  Store of Value vs. Income Generation

Bitcoin is often likened to gold because it is considered a store of value, an asset that can preserve value over time against inflation and economic uncertainties. However, unlike gold, whose history spans millennia, Bitcoin's status as a store of value is still being established. Its digital nature and the underlying blockchain technology offer a modern approach to the concept of "digital gold," appealing to those looking for alternatives to traditional financial systems and investments.

### 1.3.6.  Investment vs. Speculation

The distinction between investing and speculating is pertinent when considering Bitcoin. Investing typically involves putting capital into assets expected to generate income or grow in value due to inherent factors over time. Speculation, however, focuses on attempting to profit from market price movements, often based on short-term expectations. Bitcoin's lack of income generation places it more firmly in the realm of speculation than traditional investing.

Therefore, Bitcoin's nature as a digital currency devoid of intrinsic cash flows, speculative value, and high volatility differentiates it from traditional investments like shares or bonds. While it offers unique opportunities and challenges, Bitcoin does not provide the conventional returns associated with these older financial instruments, making it a distinct asset class with its risks and considerations.

### 1.3.7.  Proposed theory

Given the limited appealing options (speculation vs illegal bartering) for the Bitcoin. In this book, we advance the theory that **the spread of Bitcoin could have been artificially fuelled by criminals to divert attention from its true, original, and most important use** (at the core of Bitcoin), **which is the exchange of criminal activities via a medium that has been assigned a fixed value, independent of external speculation**. Transactions that occur cautiously, discreetly, and privately among criminals are never cashed out (to prevent investigators from reconstructing the audit trail). Meanwhile, all the new bitcoins mined and other excess bitcoins suffer from the volatility characterising them. Just like the float of stocks traded in the markets, whose intrinsic value, held by majority owners, is never traded.

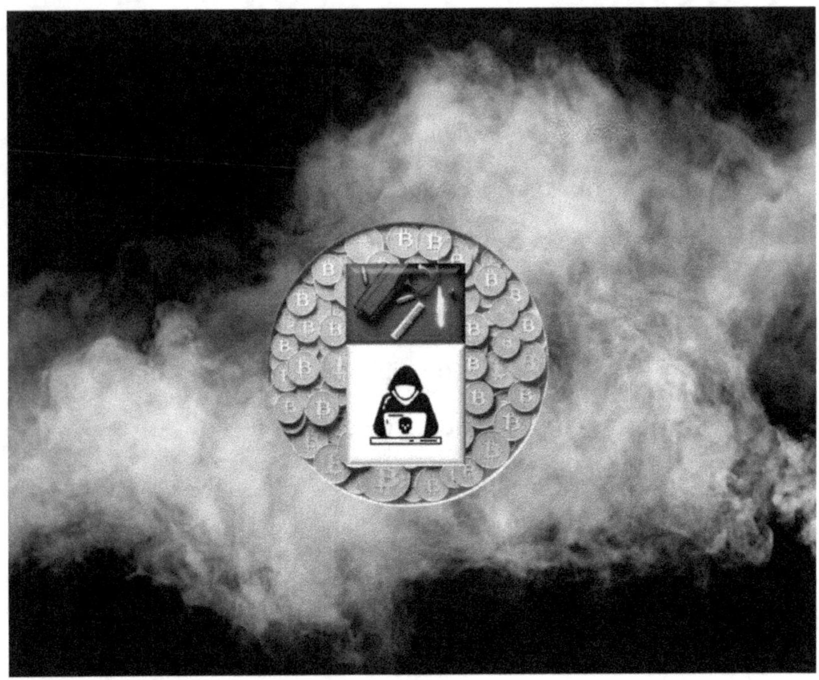

Furthermore, we have discovered that the value of transactions occurring on the dark web is always exchanged at the same conversion rate (about 20,000 USD), even when the value of Bitcoin in the market is traded at much higher values and is always subject to the volatility that distinguishes speculative investments.

Mafias are not new to attributing a fixed value to assets (preferably small ones that can anonymously enclose a high value, such as gold, diamonds, and others), similar to the value of Euro 10,000 attributed by the mafia to the Rolex Submariner (regardless of its variable market value) because it can be worn and claimed as a personal accessory not traceable to a negotiation of illegal goods.

Rolex Submariner Date 126610LN Steel Black 41 x 40mm 2023

5.0 ★ ★ ★ ★ ★ 6

**USD 14,700.00**

Rolex Submariner 41mm 124060-0001 (No Date) Black Dial, Unworn 2024

**USD 13,000.00**

Market Summary > Bitcoin

# 68,376.30 USD

+68,049.30 (20,810.18%) ↑ all time

15 Mar, 6:29 PM UTC  Disclaimer

The combination of anonymity, similar to paper money, and high-value stores (similar to diamonds, Rolex watches or gold) is a perfect mix for criminals who intend to launder money or perform illegal transactions that benefit from seamless transactions.

The following screenshot was taken on March 12, 2021, when the Bitcoin price marked one of its highest valuations (61,283.20 USD). The surprising discovery was that illegal activities on the dark web implied a conversion rate BTC of around 21,000 USD (regardless of the speculation in the market).

| Product | Price | Quantity | ₿1,00= |
|---|---|---|---|
| Remote control the phone of someone else, most new models supported | 700 USD = 0.03322 ฿ | 1 X — Buy now | $21,067 |
| Facebook and Twitter account hacking | 500 USD = 0.02373 ฿ | 1 X — Buy now | |
| Other social network account hacks, for example reddit or instagram | 450 USD = 0.02136 ฿ | 1 X — Buy now | |
| Full package deal, getting access to personal or company devices and accounts and searching for the data you need. | 1800 USD = 0.08543 ฿ | 1 X — Buy now | |
| DDOS for protected websites for 1 month | 900 USD = 0.04272 ฿ | 1 X — Buy now | |
| DDOS for unprotected websites for 1 month | 400 USD = 0.01896 ฿ | 1 X — Buy now | |
| Hacking webservers, game servers or other internet infrastructure | 1300 USD = 0.06170 ฿ | 1 X — Buy now | |
| 30 days full service, i will work 8 hours per day for 30 days only on your project | 9500 USD = 0.45088 ฿ | 1 X — Buy now | |

| Product | Price | Quantity | |
|---|---|---|---|
| FISHSCALE COCAINE 1.5g | 80 GBP = 0.00480 ฿ | 1 | X Buy now |
| FISHSCALE COCAINE 5g | 230 GBP = 0.01381 ฿ | 1 | X Buy now |
| FISHSCALE COCAINE 10g | 400 GBP = 0.02401 ฿ | 1 | X Buy now |
| PURE PLATINUM MDMA 92% 15g | 80 GBP = 0.00460 ฿ | 1 | X Buy now |
| PURE PLATINUM MDMA 92% 30g | 150 GBP = 0.00900 ฿ | 1 | X Buy now |
| PURE PLATINUM MDMA 92% 50g | 200 GBP = 0.01201 ฿ | 1 | X Buy now |
| AMNESIA HAZE - THC 21% - NEW BEST BATCH! 15g | 110 GBP = 0.00660 ฿ | 1 | X Buy now |
| AMNESIA HAZE - THC 21% - NEW BEST BATCH! 30g | 190 GBP = 0.01141 ฿ | 1 | X Buy now |
| AMNESIA HAZE - THC 21% - NEW BEST BATCH! 55g | 310 GBP = 0.01861 ฿ | 1 | X Buy now |
| ROCK ISOMER S+ KETAMINE EC 99% 7g | 100 GBP = 0.00600 ฿ | 1 | X Buy now |
| ROCK ISOMER S+ KETAMINE EC 99% 15g | 200 GBP = 0.01201 ฿ | 1 | X Buy now |

☐1,00=

£16,653 =

$21,982

| Product | Price | Quantity |
|---|---|---|
| 10 x cards with credit from 1000 to 5000 USD | 90 USD = 0.00427 ฿ | Sold out |
| 50 x cards with credit from 1000 to 5000 USD | 350 USD = 0.01661 ฿ | 1 X Buy now |
| 10 x cards with credit from 5000 to 20000 USD | 120 USD = 0.00570 ฿ | Sold out |
| 50 x cards with credit from 5000 to 20000 USD | 450 USD = 0.02136 ฿ | 1 X Buy now |
| 10 x cards with credit from 20000 to 50000 USD | 180 USD = 0.00854 ฿ | 1 X Buy now |
| 50 x cards with credit from 20000 to 50000 USD | 650 USD = 0.03085 ฿ | 1 X Buy now |
| 10 x non verified by visa cards 5000 - 100000 USD | 250 USD = 0.01187 ฿ | 1 X Buy now |
| 50 x non verified by visa cards 5000 - 100000 USD | 800 USD = 0.03797 ฿ | 1 X Buy now |

☐1,00=

$21,067

This evidence-based theory highlights criminal organisations' sophisticated use of Bitcoin and other high-value, easily transportable assets like gold and diamonds to conduct and facilitate illegal activities. Criminal networks can maintain a stable medium of exchange and value storage for transactions on the dark web and beyond by assigning a fixed value to these assets, regardless of market volatility. This system allows for the anonymous and untraceable transfer of significant value, circumventing traditional financial monitoring and law enforcement mechanisms.

Using luxury items like the Rolex Submariner as a fixed-value asset by the mafia underscores a broader strategy to leverage tangible goods as currency in the criminal underworld. This approach not only aids in laundering the proceeds of crime but also in evading the scrutiny that comes with the movement of large sums of money through conventional financial systems.

These practices underscore the challenges regulators and law enforcement face in combating the financing of illegal activities. The adaptability and innovation of criminal networks in using cryptocurrencies and luxury goods highlight the need for equally sophisticated and collaborative strategies among international law enforcement agencies, regulatory bodies, and financial institutions to address these issues. The situation calls for enhanced regulatory frameworks, improved tracking and analysis of cryptocurrency transactions, and greater cooperation across borders to disrupt the financial underpinnings of organised crime.

## 2. Anonymity Unveiled

### 2.1. The Cloak of Cryptography

Cryptography, the art of writing or solving codes, is the cornerstone of cryptocurrency anonymity. It transforms the fundamentals of financial transactions, replacing traditional identifiers with pseudonymous addresses generated through cryptographic methods. This section delves into how cryptography creates a veil of anonymity in the blockchain, the underlying technology of cryptocurrencies like Bitcoin.

#### 2.1.1. *Public and Private Keys: The Basics of Cryptocurrency Transactions*

The cryptographic system used in Bitcoin and other cryptocurrencies is based on a public key infrastructure (PKI). Each user has a pair of keys: a public key, which can be shared with others and is visible on the blockchain as a cryptocurrency address, and a private key, which is kept secret by the user. The private key is used to sign transactions, proving ownership of the funds without revealing the user's identity. The public key, derived from the private key, serves as the address to which others can send cryptocurrency.

This system ensures that the parties' identities remain obscured while transactions are visible on the blockchain. The public can see that funds have moved from one address to another, but the true identities behind those addresses remain hidden, protected by the cryptographic algorithms.

### 2.1.2.  *Hash Functions: Ensuring Integrity and Anonymity*

Hash functions are essential in maintaining the integrity and anonymity of blockchain transactions. A hash function takes input data (such as a transaction) and produces a fixed-size string of bytes, typically a digest that appears random. This process is deterministic—meaning the same input will always produce the same output—but it is practically impossible to reverse-engineer the original input from its hash output.

In the context of Bitcoin, hash functions are used to create a unique transaction identifier (TXID) and construct the blockchain itself by linking blocks via their hashes. They ensure that once a transaction is added to the blockchain, it cannot be altered without changing the entire chain, thus securing the integrity of the transaction history.

Moreover, hash functions contribute to anonymity by obscuring the transaction details. While the transaction record includes hashed information, the direct connection to the user's identity is not part of the transaction data, further enhancing privacy.

### 2.1.3.  *Limitations and Challenges*

**Despite the robust privacy features offered by cryptography, absolute anonymity is not guaranteed**. Techniques such as blockchain analysis can potentially de-anonymise users by analysing transaction patterns and network activity. Additionally, the intersection of cryptocurrencies with regulated financial systems—through exchanges and wallet services—introduces points of identity verification that can link real-world identities to cryptographic addresses.

## 2.2. Breaking the Code: Techniques for De-anonymisation

While the cryptographic foundations of Bitcoin and other cryptocurrencies offer a significant degree of privacy, the belief in their absolute anonymity is often a misconception. Advanced techniques and tools have been developed to de-anonymise blockchain transactions, peeling back the layers of privacy to reveal the identities behind cryptic transactions. This process, known as de-anonymisation or blockchain analysis, leverages the immutable and transparent nature of the blockchain against its users' privacy. Various companies and organisations have specialised in this field, each employing various approaches and techniques to trace blockchain transactions to real-world identities.

### 2.2.1.  Blockchain Analysis Companies and Their Techniques

- **Chainalysis**: is headquartered in New York, USA. Chainalysis is strategically located in one of the financial capitals of the world, positioning it close to many of its primary clients, including financial institutions and government agencies. One of the leading firms in blockchain analysis, Chainalysis provides investigative and compliance solutions to government agencies, cryptocurrency exchanges, and financial institutions. By analysing transaction patterns, identifying clusters of addresses belonging to a single entity, and using web scraping to associate information with transactions, Chainalysis helps uncover the identities behind suspicious activities.

- **Elliptic**: is based in London, UK. London's position as a global financial centre and its progressive stance towards fintech innovation make it an ideal hub for companies operating in the cryptocurrency compliance space. Specialising in identifying illicit activity on the blockchain, Elliptic uses graph analysis techniques to trace the flow of funds, detect anomalies, and flag potentially illegal transactions. Their tools can trace transactions through the blockchain's history, identifying the sources and destinations of funds, even across multiple addresses and transactions.

- **CipherTrace**: is located in Silicon Valley, California, USA. Being in the heart of technology innovation, CipherTrace benefits from proximity to tech giants and a vibrant ecosystem of startups and investors focused on blockchain and cybersecurity. CipherTrace focuses on cryptocurrency intelligence, anti-money laundering (AML) solutions, and forensics. Utilising machine learning and advanced tracing algorithms, CipherTrace analyses transaction flows, detects patterns indicative of money laundering or other illicit activities, and helps link digital identities to real-world profiles.

- **Scorechain**: is headquartered in Luxembourg. Luxembourg has a strong financial sector is known for its supportive regulatory framework for fintech companies, making it an attractive location for blockchain analytics firms. Scorechain specialises in blockchain analytics for Bitcoin and other cryptocurrencies, providing AML compliance solutions. It offers transaction monitoring and risk assessment tools that enable its users to track the origin of crypto assets and assess their risk profile based on previous activities. Scorechain's platform uses scoring algorithms to evaluate transaction histories, helping to identify high-risk transactions related to money laundering or terrorism financing.

- **Crystal Blockchain**: as a part of Bitfury, Crystal Blockchain operates under the umbrella of a company with a global presence. Bitfury, headquartered in Amsterdam, Netherlands, has offices and operations in several countries, highlighting its international reach. Developed by Bitfury, Crystal Blockchain offers comprehensive blockchain analytics solutions, including monitoring and risk scoring of cryptocurrency transactions. Its platform is designed to provide detailed transaction analysis, including the ability to identify connections between cryptocurrency wallets and known illicit entities. Crystal Blockchain employs clustering algorithms to aggregate related addresses, enhancing the ability to trace suspicious activities through complex chains of transactions.

- **Coinfirm**: based in London, UK, with additional offices in Poland. Like Elliptic, Coinfirm's presence in London allows it to engage closely with the European financial market and regulatory landscape. Coinfirm offers an AML platform designed to streamline compliance with regulations related to cryptocurrencies and blockchain. The platform utilises big data analysis and algorithms to provide risk assessments of blockchain transactions. Coinfirm's AML platform can detect patterns and behaviours associated with money laundering, ransomware activity, and other financial crimes, offering a detailed risk score for each assessed transaction.

- **Neutrino (acquired by Coinbase)**: Before its acquisition by Coinbase, Neutrino was headquartered in Milan, Italy. Coinbase, one of the largest cryptocurrency exchanges, is based in San Francisco, California, USA. The acquisition has likely integrated Neutrino's operations into Coinbase's global presence. Neutrino's technology focuses on monitoring blockchain networks for transactions associated with illicit activities. Its platform offers tools for tracking the flow of assets across multiple blockchains, detecting suspicious patterns, and identifying high-risk addresses. By analysing the blockchain with advanced algorithms, Neutrino helps exchanges, wallet providers, and financial institutions mitigate risks associated with cryptocurrency transactions.

- **TRM Labs**: is based in San Francisco, California, USA. Like CipherTrace, its location in Silicon Valley offers strategic advantages regarding access to technology resources and talent in the blockchain and fintech sectors. TRM Labs provides blockchain intelligence solutions to combat cryptocurrency fraud and financial crimes. Its platform leverages artificial intelligence and blockchain analysis techniques to monitor real-time transactions, identify risk indicators, and trace the flow of funds across blockchain networks. TRM Labs' tools aim to enable compliance with regulatory requirements and protect against exposure to illicit activities in the crypto space.

- **Whitestream**: is an Israeli blockchain analytics company. Israel's major tech hubs include Tel Aviv, known for its vibrant startup ecosystem, and Herzliya, home to numerous high-tech companies. Given the nature of tech companies in Israel, it is likely that Whitestream operates out of one of these cities or another major tech centre in the country. Whitestream is an Israeli blockchain analytics company that provides intelligence and anti-money laundering (AML) services focused on the cryptocurrency industry. They offer solutions for monitoring blockchain transactions to identify and track suspicious activities, enhancing security and compliance within the crypto space.

- **Firmo (acquired by eToro)**: Firmo was also based in Israel before its acquisition. eToro itself is headquartered in Tel Aviv, Israel. Tel Aviv is a leading city in technological innovation and finance, making it a fitting location for a company like eToro that merges financial services with new tech. After the acquisition, Firmo's technology and team became part of eToro, further contributing to eToro's offerings from its base in Tel Aviv. While Firmo's primary focus was on smart contract development for financial derivatives on various blockchains, its acquisition by eToro, a social trading and investment platform headquartered in Israel, underscores the country's involvement in broader aspects of blockchain technology and financial innovation.

### 2.2.2. *Techniques for De-anonymisation*

- **Cluster Analysis**: one common technique is cluster analysis, where multiple addresses are identified as controlled by a single entity. This method relies on patterns such as addresses being inputs in the same transaction, suggesting ownership by a single entity.

- **Transaction Pattern Analysis**: by examining the timing, amount, and frequency of transactions, analysts can identify patterns that may tie anonymous blockchain activity to specific behaviours or identities.

- **Network Analysis**: analysing the network of transactions allows for identifying central nodes, which can be exchanges, wallet providers, or other financial services. These nodes often have Know Your Customer (KYC) information that can link blockchain addresses to real identities.

- **Fiat On/Off Ramps Analysis**: Converting cryptocurrency to fiat currency (cashing out) or vice versa often requires using exchanges and implementing KYC policies. It necessitates the provision of identification documents, creating a link between the blockchain address and the individual's real-world identity.

- **CoinJoin Detection**: CoinJoin is a method used to increase privacy by combining multiple Bitcoin payments from multiple spenders into a single transaction, making it more difficult to determine who paid whom. Detecting CoinJoin transactions and analysing them involves advanced pattern recognition algorithms that can identify the common characteristics of these transactions despite their designed anonymity.

- **Dusting Attacks**: A dusting attack involves sending small amounts of cryptocurrency, known as "dust," to many addresses. By tracking the movement of these dust transactions, analysts can potentially de-anonymise users when these small amounts are consolidated with larger transactions, revealing ownership patterns.

- **Temporal Analysis**: This technique examines the timing of transactions to correlate blockchain activity with real-world events or specific time zones. Temporal analysis can help infer users' location or tie their online activity to physical identities based on when transactions occur.

- **Social Network Analysis (SNA)**: SNA goes beyond the blockchain to incorporate external data sources, such as social media, forums, and dark web marketplaces. Analysts can identify user relationships and potentially uncover real identities by linking information shared in these platforms with blockchain transactions.

- **Wallet Software Fingerprinting**: Different cryptocurrency wallet applications can leave specific "fingerprints" in transaction patterns, fee structures, or other unique characteristics. Analysing these fingerprints can help identify the wallet software used for a transaction and potentially link it to groups or individuals.

- **Heuristic-Based Tagging**: This approach involves creating heuristics or rules based on known behaviours of illicit transactions. For example, transactions that move funds through privacy-enhancing services or across jurisdictions in a pattern typical of money laundering can be flagged for further investigation.

### 2.2.3. *Anonymity Misconception*

The misconception of Bitcoin's anonymity largely stems from its early days, where the novelty of blockchain technology and the lack of sophisticated analysis tools allowed for greater privacy. However, as the ecosystem has matured, so have the methods for de-anonymising transactions. The immutable and transparent nature of the blockchain means that once a link between an address and an identity is established, the entire transaction history of that address becomes traceable.

The process of cashing out further complicates the notion of anonymity. Converting Bitcoin to fiat currency typically requires interaction with a financial institution or exchange, most of which are bound by regulatory requirements to implement stringent AML and KYC procedures. It creates a documented link between the transaction history on the blockchain and the individual's identity, effectively lifting the veil of anonymity.

Trading Bitcoin and other cryptocurrencies carries a unique set of risks, including the potential for frozen or confiscated assets while converting cryptocurrencies into fiat currency, especially if those assets are connected with illicit activities such as ransomware attacks. This risk stems from the traceability of transactions on the blockchain and the rigorous anti-money laundering (AML) and know-your-customer (KYC) regulations that financial institutions, including cryptocurrency exchanges, must adhere to.

### 2.2.4. Traceability and Regulation

The blockchain's transparent ledger ensures that all transactions are permanently recorded and openly accessible. While this promotes transparency and security, it also allows tracing funds back through the transaction history. Using advanced blockchain analysis tools, law enforcement and regulatory agencies can track the movement of cryptocurrencies involved in or resulting from illegal activities.

When these traced cryptocurrencies interact with regulated financial entities, such as exchanges or banks, the funds involved can be identified as connected to illicit activities. Financial institutions have legal obligations to report suspicious activities and implement AML measures. As part of these obligations, they may freeze or confiscate funds suspected of being involved in crimes, such as ransomware payments, to comply with legal and regulatory mandates.

### 2.2.5. Risk to Innocent Traders

For traders and investors, the interconnectedness of blockchain transactions means that even those not directly involved in illegal activities can be impacted. If you receive or trade Bitcoin previously used in a ransomware attack, your assets could be flagged as suspicious when you attempt to cash out or convert them into fiat currency through a regulated exchange. The exchange, acting in compliance with AML regulations and law enforcement directives, may freeze your assets and, in some cases, confiscate them pending an investigation.

This scenario poses a significant risk, as individuals may unknowingly come into possession of tainted coins, especially in a market where the average user does not commonly scrutinise each cryptocurrency unit's history. Cryptocurrencies' decentralised and pseudonymous nature makes it challenging for individuals to fully ascertain their digital assets' history.

### 2.2.6.  Mitigation Strategies

To mitigate these risks, individuals can take several precautions when trading or investing in cryptocurrencies:

- **Use Reputable Exchanges**: Trade and cash out your cryptocurrencies through reputable exchanges with robust AML and KYC procedures. It can reduce the risk of becoming inadvertently involved in the transaction of tainted assets.

- **Practice Due Diligence**: Where possible, conduct due diligence on the transaction history of cryptocurrencies you acquire, especially if they come from direct peer-to-peer transactions or less reputable sources.

- **Stay Informed**: Keep informed about best practices for cryptocurrency security and legal developments related to cryptocurrency regulation.

- **Use Mixing Services with Caution**: While mixing services can obfuscate the history of cryptocurrencies, they can also raise red flags with regulators due to their association with attempts to launder money. Their use should be carefully considered.

### 2.3. The Audit Trail: Tracking Transactions in the Blockchain

The blockchain's inherent design facilitates the transfer of digital assets and ensures that every transaction is recorded in a verifiable, immutable ledger. This characteristic is pivotal for creating an audit trail, a comprehensive record that offers transparency and accountability for all transactions conducted on the blockchain. The audit trail feature of blockchain technology has profound implications for financial transparency, regulatory compliance, and the detection of illicit activities.

#### 2.3.1.    Immutable Record-Keeping

At the heart of the blockchain's audit trail capability is its immutability. Once a transaction is confirmed and added to a block, it cannot be altered or deleted, ensuring that every transaction is permanently recorded. This immutability is safeguarded by cryptographic hashes, which link each block to its predecessor in a tamper-evident chain. As a result, the blockchain serves as an incontrovertible record of all transactions, accessible to anyone with permission to view the ledger.

#### 2.3.2.    Enhancing Transparency and Trust

The transparency afforded by blockchain's audit trail enhances trust among participants. Central authorities like banks or governments often mediate trust in traditional financial systems. In contrast, blockchain technology decentralises trust, allowing parties to transact directly with one another with the confidence that their transaction records are secure, accurate, and unchangeable. This level of transparency is particularly appealing in applications where data integrity is critical, such as supply chain management, voting systems, and financial services.

### 2.3.3. Facilitating Regulatory Compliance

For regulators and compliance officers, the blockchain's audit trail provides a powerful tool for overseeing financial transactions. The ability to trace the flow of assets across the blockchain enables the detection of anomalous or illegal activities, such as money laundering, fraud, and terrorist financing. Regulatory bodies can use blockchain analysis tools to review transaction histories, verify the legitimacy of asset transfers, and ensure that entities comply with anti-money laundering (AML) and know-your-customer (KYC) regulations.

### 2.3.4. Challenges and Considerations

While the audit trail feature of the blockchain offers significant benefits, it also presents challenges. The pseudonymous nature of blockchain transactions means that, while the flow of assets can be traced, linking transactions to real-world identities requires additional information or analysis. As discussed previously, it has led to the development of advanced de-anonymisation techniques that strive to balance privacy concerns with the need for transparency and regulatory oversight.

Moreover, the sheer volume of data on public blockchains can make auditing and analysis complex and resource-intensive. Developing efficient and effective tools for blockchain analysis is an ongoing area of innovation, aiming to make the audit trail more accessible and useful for various stakeholders.

### 3.  Bitcoin as the People's Money

The advent of Bitcoin and its ascent in the digital era have sparked a global conversation about the nature of money, value, and the control systems governing financial transactions. In this discourse, Robert Kiyosaki, a prominent financial educator and author of "Rich Dad Poor Dad," presents a compelling narrative that categorises money into three distinct types: Gold as "God's Money," Bitcoin as "The People's Money," and fiat currencies as "Fake Money." Kiyosaki's classification sheds light on the evolving perceptions of value and trust in the modern economy.

#### 3.1. From Concept to Reality: Bitcoin in the Words of Robert Kiyosaki

Kiyosaki's endorsement of Bitcoin focuses on its characteristic as a form of "people's money" – a decentralised and borderless digital asset that stands apart from the traditional financial systems and their susceptibility to inflation, government control, and financial manipulation. Despite Bitcoin's notorious volatility, Kiyosaki and many like him see it more as a store of value, akin to gold, rather than a conventional investment vehicle that yields returns through dividends or interest.

#### 3.2. Bitcoin as a Storage of Value

The concept of Bitcoin as a storage of value rather than an investment hinges on several factors:

- **Decentralisation and Limited Supply**: Bitcoin operates on a decentralised network, free from central authority control, and has a capped supply of 21 million coins. Much like gold, this scarcity underpins its value proposition as a hedge against inflation and the devaluation of fiat currencies, which can be printed without limit.

- **Volatility and Maturation**: While Bitcoin's volatility is often cited as a drawback, it reflects the asset's relative infancy and the growing pains of gaining acceptance of a new form of money. Over time, as adoption increases and the market matures, many proponents argue that Bitcoin's price will stabilise, solidifying its role as a store of value.

- **Comparisons with Gold and Fiat Currency**: Kiyosaki's analogy positions gold as a timeless store of value ("God's Money"), recognised and revered across civilisations. Fiat currencies, by contrast, are labelled as "Fake Money" due to their lack of intrinsic value and susceptibility to inflation. With its fixed supply and independence from traditional financial systems, Bitcoin is envisioned as "The People's Money" – accessible, equitable, and designed for the digital age.

### 3.2.1. Challenges and Considerations

The view of Bitcoin as a storage of value rather than an investment raises important considerations:

- **Acceptance and Utility**: For Bitcoin to fully realise its potential as "The People's Money," it must achieve widespread acceptance, not just as an asset to hold but also as a medium of exchange for goods and services.

- **Regulatory Environment**: The regulatory landscape will play a pivotal role in shaping Bitcoin's future, influencing its adoption, use cases, and perception among the public.

- **Technological Evolution**: Ongoing technological improvements, such as enhancements in scalability and security, are crucial for Bitcoin to support its growing user base and expand its utility beyond being a mere store of value.

## 3.3. The Ideological Divide: Bitcoin vs Traditional Banking

The rise of Bitcoin has catalysed a profound ideological divide between the ethos of decentralised digital currencies and the principles underpinning traditional banking systems. This divide is not merely about the choice of financial instruments but represents a fundamental disagreement over the control, accessibility, and future direction of financial systems globally.

### 3.3.1. Centralisation vs Decentralisation

At the heart of this divide is the contrast between the centralisation inherent in traditional banking and the decentralisation championed by Bitcoin and other cryptocurrencies. Traditional banking systems operate within a framework controlled by central authorities—central banks, financial institutions, or government bodies. These entities regulate the flow of money, dictate monetary policy, and have the authority to influence the economy through interest rates, lending practices, and quantitative easing.

Bitcoin, by contrast, operates on a decentralised network, relying on blockchain technology to distribute control across its users. This decentralisation means no single entity can control Bitcoin's supply transactions or dictate its value. The democratic nature of Bitcoin's blockchain offers a stark alternative to the hierarchical structures of traditional banking, proposing a system where transparency, equality, and direct peer-to-peer transactions prevail.

### 3.3.2. *Trust and Transparency*

Traditional banking systems are built on the concept of trust in centralised institutions to manage and safeguard the public's financial assets. However, financial crises, bank failures, and instances of fraud have eroded public trust in these institutions, highlighting their vulnerabilities and the potential for systemic risk.

Bitcoin introduces a trustless system, where trust is placed not in a central authority but in cryptography, consensus mechanisms, and the immutable nature of the blockchain. Every transaction is transparently recorded on the blockchain and accessible to anyone, ensuring transparency and auditability without intermediaries.

### 3.3.3. *Accessibility and Inclusion*

Traditional banking often fails to serve the unbanked or underbanked populations, particularly in developing regions, due to barriers such as lack of documentation, financial literacy, or physical access to banking facilities. Bitcoin and cryptocurrencies offer a potential solution to this issue, providing universal access to financial services through the internet. This accessibility promises a more inclusive financial system where anyone with an internet connection can participate in the global economy, regardless of geographical location or socio-economic status.

### 3.3.4. *The Future of Finance*

The ideological divide between Bitcoin and traditional banking also encompasses differing visions for the future of finance. Advocates of Bitcoin envisage a world where financial sovereignty is restored to individuals, reducing reliance on potentially unstable fiat currencies and offering protection against inflation and governmental mismanagement. In contrast, proponents of traditional banking systems argue for the stability, security, and regulatory oversight established financial institutions provide, viewing them as essential for economic growth and financial security.

### 3.4. Empowerment Through Decentralisation

The decentralisation inherent in Bitcoin and other cryptocurrencies represents a technological innovation and a paradigm shift in how financial power and control are distributed. This shift from centralised financial systems towards a more decentralised model promises to redefine the landscape of financial empowerment, offering new opportunities for individual autonomy, financial inclusion, and resistance against inflation and financial instability.

#### 3.4.1. Financial Autonomy and Control

One of the most compelling aspects of decentralisation is the empowerment it offers individuals over their financial assets. In traditional banking systems, individuals entrust their money to institutions susceptible to economic downturns, mismanagement, or expropriation through bank bail-ins or inflationary policies. Decentralised cryptocurrencies like Bitcoin place the control back into the hands of the individual, enabling people to hold, transact, and manage their wealth independently of traditional financial intermediaries.

This empowerment is particularly poignant in scenarios where trust in national currencies or banks is low, whether due to hyperinflation, economic instability, or political unrest. By providing an alternative store of value and means of transaction, Bitcoin offers a form of financial sovereignty that can be especially valuable in countries with restrictive financial systems or unstable fiat currencies.

### 3.4.2. *Financial Inclusion and Global Accessibility*

Decentralisation also plays a crucial role in enhancing financial inclusion. Approximately 1.7 billion adults worldwide lack access to traditional banking services, often due to geographical barriers, lack of documentation, or minimum balance requirements. Decentralised cryptocurrencies, accessible to anyone with an internet connection, offer a gateway to financial services for the unbanked and underbanked populations.

This accessibility means that individuals can participate in the global economy, send and receive payments, and access savings and credit facilities without needing a bank account. Such inclusion empowers individuals economically and can drive broader economic development and participation in regions previously marginalised from the financial system.

### 3.4.3. *Resistance Against Inflation and Financial Instability*

With their capped supply and independence from central bank policies, decentralised currencies like Bitcoin offer a hedge against inflation and financial instability. Traditional fiat currencies can lose value over time due to inflationary monetary policies or economic downturns. In contrast, Bitcoin's supply is algorithmically limited to 21 million coins, making it deflationary by design.

This characteristic makes Bitcoin and similar cryptocurrencies attractive as long-term stores of value, akin to digital gold. For individuals in countries experiencing high inflation rates, Bitcoin provides an alternative means to preserve purchasing power and protect savings from devaluation, further enhancing financial empowerment.

### 3.4.4. *Challenges and the Path Forward*

While empowerment through decentralisation presents significant opportunities, it also comes with challenges. Regulatory uncertainties, market volatility, and technological barriers to entry can obstruct the widespread adoption of cryptocurrencies. Moreover, the responsibility for security and asset management shifts to the individual, requiring a certain level of technological proficiency and awareness of cybersecurity risks.

Despite these challenges, the movement towards decentralisation continues to gain momentum, driven by the potential for greater financial empowerment, inclusion, and stability it offers. As technology evolves and awareness grows, the barriers to participation may diminish, paving the way for a more inclusive, empowered, and decentralised financial future.

## 4. A Regulatory Maze

### 4.1. The Evolution of Bitcoin Regulation

#### 4.1.1. Early Days: A Regulatory Void

There was a virtual regulatory void in the early days following Bitcoin's creation in 2009. Governments and financial authorities worldwide were largely unaware of or indifferent to cryptocurrencies. This lack of regulation allowed the ecosystem to grow organically, ensuring innovation and adoption and leading to notable instances of fraud, hacks, and illicit use cases such as the Silk Road marketplace.

#### 4.1.2. Waking Up to Bitcoin: Initial Reactions

As Bitcoin gained in value and prominence, regulators began to take notice. Initial reactions varied widely:

- **Bans and Restrictions**: Some countries, wary of the potential for money laundering, tax evasion, and loss of monetary control, chose to ban or restrict cryptocurrency activities. For example, Bangladesh and Bolivia implemented early bans on Bitcoin and other cryptocurrencies.

- **Warnings and Guidance**: Other jurisdictions warned consumers about the risks associated with cryptocurrencies, including volatility, security risks, and the lack of regulatory protection. These warnings often came with a wait-and-see approach to regulation, allowing the market to develop further before deciding on a specific regulatory strategy.

### 4.1.3. *Towards a Framework for Regulation*

The need for a more structured regulatory approach became apparent as the cryptocurrency market matured. It led to several key developments:

- **Anti-Money Laundering (AML) and Know Your Customer (KYC)**: One of the first focus areas for regulators was incorporating cryptocurrencies into existing AML and KYC frameworks. The Financial Action Task Force (FATF), an international body setting standards for combating money laundering, began issuing guidance on how countries should regulate cryptocurrencies to prevent their use in illicit finance.

- **Securities and Investment Laws**: The initial coin offerings (ICOs) explosion in 2017 further complicated the regulatory landscape, as authorities had to determine whether cryptocurrencies and related products should be classified as securities. It led to regulatory actions in countries like the United States, where the Securities and Exchange Commission (SEC) began cracking down on unregistered ICOs.

- **Taxation**: Countries also started to clarify the tax treatment of cryptocurrencies. For instance, the Internal Revenue Service (IRS) in the United States classified Bitcoin as property for tax purposes, requiring capital gains tax on cryptocurrency transactions.

### 4.1.4.  *The Current State: A Patchwork of Regulation*

Today, the regulatory environment for Bitcoin and cryptocurrencies remains a patchwork of national and regional laws. Some countries, like Japan and Switzerland, have created welcoming regulatory environments to attract crypto businesses, while others, like China, have taken a more restrictive stance, especially regarding cryptocurrency exchanges and ICOs.

Despite these differences, a common theme in many jurisdictions is the recognition of the need to balance innovation with consumer protection, financial stability, and the prevention of criminal activity. It has led to ongoing dialogue between regulators, industry participants, and stakeholders to refine and adapt regulatory frameworks to cryptocurrencies' unique challenges and opportunities.

## 4.2. Global Perspectives on Cryptocurrency Oversight

Countries grapple with the dual challenge of ensuring innovation and financial stability, and the regulatory stance on cryptocurrencies varies widely across jurisdictions. This section explores global perspectives on cryptocurrency oversight, highlighting key examples of regulatory approaches.

### 4.2.1.  Embracing Cryptocurrencies: Japan and Switzerland

- **Japan**: Recognised as one of the first countries to fully embrace cryptocurrencies, Japan made Bitcoin a legal payment method in 2017. The country's Financial Services Agency (FSA) oversees the registration and compliance of cryptocurrency exchanges, promoting a secure and vibrant crypto ecosystem. Japan's progressive stance is partly driven by its aim to become a global leader in fintech, although it maintains strict regulatory oversight to prevent money laundering and fraud.

- **Switzerland**: Known for its financial privacy and innovation-friendly environment, Switzerland has emerged as a cryptocurrency and blockchain technology hub. The Swiss Financial Market Supervisory Authority (FINMA) has provided clear guidelines for ICOs and digital currencies, distinguishing between payment, utility, and asset tokens. The "Crypto Valley" in Zug is a testament to Switzerland's welcoming stance, housing numerous blockchain startups and initiatives.

*4.2.2. Regulatory Caution: United States and European Union*

- **United States**: The U.S. presents a complex regulatory environment due to its multiple regulatory bodies with overlapping jurisdictions. The Securities and Exchange Commission (SEC) regulates digital assets deemed as securities, while the Commodity Futures Trading Commission (CFTC) considers cryptocurrencies like Bitcoin commodities. The Internal Revenue Service (IRS) treats cryptocurrencies as property for tax purposes. This fragmented regulatory approach reflects caution and a focus on protecting investors from risks associated with digital assets.

- **European Union**: The EU has been working towards harmonising cryptocurrency regulation among its member states. The Fifth Anti-Money Laundering Directive (5AMLD) enhanced transparency by including cryptocurrency exchanges and wallet providers under the EU's anti-money laundering regulations. The proposed Markets in Crypto-Assets (MiCA) framework aims to provide comprehensive oversight of the crypto sector, ensuring consumer protection and financial stability across the EU.

*4.2.3. Restrictive Approaches: China and India*

- **China**: Once a global leader in cryptocurrency trading and mining, China has taken a more restrictive stance in recent years. The Chinese government has banned ICOs, shut down local cryptocurrency exchanges, and restricted access to foreign exchanges to curb what it perceives as financial risks associated with cryptocurrencies. Despite this, China is actively exploring the potential of blockchain technology and developing its digital currency, the Digital Currency Electronic Payment (DCEP).

- **India**: India's approach to cryptocurrency regulation has seen shifts over the years. The Reserve Bank of India (RBI) had effectively banned cryptocurrency transactions through regulated financial institutions, but the Supreme Court of India overturned this ban in 2020, citing disproportionality. Despite the legal victory, the Indian government continues to express concerns over cryptocurrencies, proposing legislation that could impose further restrictions.

The relationship between cryptocurrencies, anti-money laundering (AML) measures, terrorism financing, and global sanctions is complex and increasingly significant in the global financial landscape. As digital currencies like Bitcoin have grown in popularity, they have presented opportunities and challenges for regulatory and enforcement agencies worldwide. The pseudonymous nature of transactions, the decentralised structure of networks, and the global reach of cryptocurrencies have necessitated the development and adaptation of AML frameworks to address these new vectors for potential misuse.

**Anti-Money Laundering (AML)**

Cryptocurrencies have been scrutinised for their potential use in money laundering activities due to their ability to transact semi-anonymously across borders without traditional oversight in the banking sector. In response, international and national regulatory bodies have extended AML regulations to cover cryptocurrency transactions:

- **The Financial Action Task Force (FATF)** has issued guidance for member countries to regulate virtual asset service providers (VASPs), including cryptocurrency exchanges, with AML and counter-terrorism financing (CTF) measures akin to those applied to traditional financial institutions. It includes the requirement for VASPs to implement Know Your Customer (KYC) procedures, monitor suspicious activities, and report to the relevant authorities.

- **National Regulations**: Following the FATF's recommendations, countries worldwide have begun incorporating cryptocurrency transactions into their AML legislation. It requires exchanges to register with financial authorities, perform customer due diligence, and report suspicious transactions.

*4.2.4.  Terrorism Financing*

Cryptocurrencies in terrorism financing remain a concern for governments due to the perceived difficulty in tracing transactions. Terrorist groups may use cryptocurrencies to raise funds anonymously through donations or to move money across borders without detection. In response, efforts to de-anonymise blockchain transactions through advanced analysis tools and techniques have intensified, aiming to track the flow of funds and uncover the networks behind these activities.

### 4.2.5. *Global Sanctions*

Cryptocurrencies also pose challenges for the enforcement of global sanctions. Individuals or entities targeted by sanctions can potentially use cryptocurrencies to evade restrictions on accessing the international financial system or to fund activities in violation of sanctions covertly. As a result:

- **Sanctions Lists**: Regulatory bodies, especially in the United States, like the Office of Foreign Assets Control (OFAC), have started including digital currency addresses associated with sanctioned individuals or entities. It is aimed at preventing them from using cryptocurrencies to circumvent sanctions.

- **International Cooperation**: The effective enforcement of sanctions in cryptocurrencies requires international cooperation, given the borderless nature of digital transactions. Information sharing and joint efforts among countries are crucial to identifying and blocking transactions related to sanctioned entities.

## 5.  The Road to Acceptability

Bitcoin's journey towards mainstream adoption is a narrative of resilience, innovation, and an evolving understanding of what constitutes money in the digital age. Once regarded as a niche interest for tech enthusiasts and libertarians, Bitcoin has progressively cemented its place within the broader financial ecosystem, challenging traditional notions of currency and asset class.

### 5.1. Bitcoin's Journey to Mainstream Adoption

#### 5.1.1.  *Early Days and the Cypherpunk Vision*

Bitcoin's inception in 2009 was deeply rooted in the cypherpunk ethos—a vision for using cryptography to bring about social and political change, particularly in creating financial privacy and security. Initially, Bitcoin was primarily of interest within these circles, seen as an experiment in creating a decentralised currency outside the control of any government or central authority.

#### 5.1.2.  *Gaining Recognition: From Silk Road to Wall Street*

The path to acceptance began in the shadows; Bitcoin first gained widespread attention as the currency of choice on the Silk Road, an online black market, highlighting its potential for anonymity and resistance to censorship. While this association with illicit activities initially cast a shadow over Bitcoin, it also demonstrated the robustness of its underlying technology, drawing curiosity from a broader audience.

The turning point for Bitcoin's journey to mainstream adoption was its gradual recognition by the financial industry and investors. As Bitcoin's price experienced significant volatility but an overall upward trajectory, it caught the eye of both retail and institutional investors. High-profile endorsements, public investments by corporations, and the launch of Bitcoin futures contracts by major financial exchanges signified a shift in perception, with Bitcoin beginning to be seen as a legitimate investment and a "digital gold" hedge against inflation.

### 5.1.3. *Technological Advancements and Scaling Solutions*

For Bitcoin to gain mainstream acceptance, it needed to address significant challenges, particularly scalability, transaction fees, and processing times. Implementing the Lightning Network, a second-layer protocol that enables off-chain transactions, and improvements in blockchain technology have been crucial in addressing these issues, making Bitcoin more practical for everyday transactions and micro-payments.

### 5.1.4. *Regulatory Clarity and Institutional Adoption*

Regulatory uncertainty is one of the most significant hurdles to Bitcoin's acceptability. However, in recent years, regulatory bodies worldwide have moved towards greater clarity and acceptance. The approval of Bitcoin ETFs (exchange-traded funds) in several countries, integrating Bitcoin into traditional banking services, and developing regulatory frameworks specifically for cryptocurrencies have helped legitimise Bitcoin as an asset class.

Moreover, the adoption of Bitcoin by major companies, both as an asset on their balance sheets and as a payment method, along with endorsements from well-known public figures in the financial world, has further reinforced its legitimacy and potential for widespread use.

### 5.1.5.  *Global Acceptance and the Future*

The ultimate testament to Bitcoin's journey towards mainstream adoption is its growing acceptance as a form of payment and store of value across the globe. Countries like El Salvador have taken bold steps by adopting Bitcoin as a legal tender, which, while controversial, marks a significant milestone in Bitcoin's acceptance.

## 5.2. El Salvador: The First Domino to Fall

El Salvador's unprecedented move to adopt Bitcoin as legal tender has created global ripples, prompting other nations to reevaluate their stance on cryptocurrencies. While the full impact of this decision is yet to be seen, it has undeniably sparked a renewed interest in the potential applications of Bitcoin and other digital currencies in national economies. This section explores the varying responses from other countries and the potential for a broader shift towards accepting cryptocurrencies.

### 5.2.1. Increased Interest in Cryptocurrencies

Following El Salvador's lead, several countries have shown increased interest in exploring the possibilities of cryptocurrencies:

- **Central and South America**: Nations such as Panama, Paraguay, and Brazil have seen proposals and discussions among lawmakers and government officials about embracing Bitcoin and other digital currencies, either as legal tender or through regulatory frameworks that encourage their use.

- **Caribbean**: The Bahamas has launched its digital currency, the Sand Dollar, to enhance financial inclusion and reduce operational costs. Similarly, other Caribbean nations are exploring digital currencies to bolster their financial systems and attract digital nomads and fintech businesses.

- **Africa and Asia**: Countries with significant unbanked populations and high remittance inflows, such as Nigeria and the Philippines, are examining the role of digital currencies in their economies. Nigeria, for instance, has launched its own central bank digital currency (CBDC), the eNaira, as a step towards adopting digital financial solutions.

### 5.2.2.  Regulatory and Legislative Developments

The response to El Salvador's Bitcoin adoption has also accelerated regulatory and legislative efforts in various countries, aiming to provide clearer frameworks for the use and trading of cryptocurrencies:

- **Regulatory Clarity**: Nations increasingly recognise the need for regulatory clarity around cryptocurrencies to protect consumers, prevent financial crimes, and foster innovation. It includes developing guidelines for cryptocurrency exchanges, ICOs, and tax treatments of digital assets.

- **Central Bank Digital Currencies (CBDCs)**: The concept of CBDCs has gained momentum, with countries like China, the European Union, and Canada exploring or developing their digital currencies. These initiatives reflect an interest in leveraging blockchain technology for digital money, albeit in a more controlled and centralised manner than decentralised cryptocurrencies like Bitcoin.

### 5.2.3.  Challenges and Considerations

As countries explore the potential adoption or regulation of cryptocurrencies, several challenges and considerations emerge:

- **Volatility and Stability**: Concerns about the volatility of cryptocurrencies like Bitcoin remain a significant barrier to their adoption as legal tender or mainstream financial instruments.

- **Financial Inclusion vs. Financial Stability**: While digital currencies offer a promising solution to financial inclusion, regulators must balance these benefits against financial stability and integrity risks.

- **International Cooperation**: The global nature of cryptocurrencies necessitates international cooperation and coordination in regulatory approaches to prevent regulatory arbitrage and ensure effective oversight of cross-border cryptocurrency transactions.

Caribbean countries have shown a growing interest in Bitcoin and other cryptocurrencies for several reasons, reflecting the region's unique economic, financial, and social conditions. The adoption and exploration of digital currencies in these countries are driven by factors that enhance financial inclusion, attract investment, and leverage technology for economic development. Here are some key reasons why Caribbean countries are drawn to Bitcoin and cryptocurrencies:

### 5.2.4. Financial Inclusion

A significant portion of the population in Caribbean countries is unbanked or underbanked, lacking access to traditional banking services. Cryptocurrencies like Bitcoin offer a promising solution by enabling secure, low-cost financial transactions accessible via smartphones and the internet. It can dramatically improve access to financial services for remote or underserved communities, facilitating savings, payments, and remittances without physical bank branches.

### 5.2.5. Remittances

Remittances play a crucial role in the economies of many Caribbean nations, with a substantial amount of their GDP coming from funds sent home by expatriates. Traditional remittance channels often come with high fees and slow processing times. Bitcoin and other cryptocurrencies can offer a more efficient and cost-effective way of sending remittances, reducing transaction costs and increasing the amount of money reaching recipients.

### 5.2.6. Economic Resilience and Diversification

Caribbean economies, often reliant on tourism and exports, face vulnerabilities to external shocks such as natural disasters, global economic downturns, and pandemics. Cryptocurrencies offer a pathway to economic diversification and resilience. By embracing digital currencies and blockchain technology, Caribbean countries can attract investment in the fintech sector, create jobs, and foster economic growth beyond traditional industries.

### 5.2.7. Attracting Digital Nomads and Fintech Investment

Several Caribbean countries are positioning themselves as attractive destinations for digital nomads and fintech companies by adopting crypto-friendly policies. By creating a regulatory environment supporting cryptocurrency and blockchain innovation, these countries aim to become hubs for digital finance, attracting talent, technology, and capital to spur economic development.

### 5.2.8. *Sovereignty and Reduced Dependence on Foreign Currencies*

Foreign currencies like the US dollar are common in the Caribbean for trade and savings. However, reliance on foreign currencies comes with challenges, including exposure to exchange rate risk and monetary policy decisions made outside the region. Cryptocurrencies offer an alternative that can help reduce dependence on foreign currencies and give Caribbean nations more control over their financial systems.

### 5.2.9. *Regulatory Innovation*

Some Caribbean nations are leading in regulatory innovation concerning cryptocurrencies. For example, Bermuda has established a comprehensive regulatory framework for digital assets, covering ICOs, digital asset businesses, and banks dealing in cryptocurrencies. These regulatory efforts aim to ensure consumer protection while fostering an environment conducive to digital finance innovation.

## 5.3. The Ripple Effect: Other Nations and Bitcoin

El Salvador's landmark decision to adopt Bitcoin as legal tender has generated widespread international interest, setting off what could be described as a "ripple effect" across the globe. This move has prompted other nations to re-evaluate their stance on Bitcoin and cryptocurrencies more broadly, exploring the potential benefits and challenges of greater integration into their financial systems. Below, we examine the varied reactions from different countries and regions, highlighting how El Salvador's decision might influence the future trajectory of Bitcoin and cryptocurrency acceptance worldwide.

### 5.3.1. Latin America's Growing Enthusiasm

Following El Salvador's announcement, several countries in Latin America have shown increased interest in Bitcoin and cryptocurrencies:

- **Panama** introduced a bill aiming to legalise Bitcoin and other cryptocurrencies, focusing on innovation, digital transformation, and the goal of becoming a hub for technology and financial services.

- **Paraguay** has seen proposals from its lawmakers to draft cryptocurrency legislation that could make the country more crypto-friendly, though it stops short of adopting Bitcoin as legal tender.

- **Brazil** and **Argentina** have witnessed growing public and institutional interest in cryptocurrencies. In Brazil, several

bills related to cryptocurrencies are under discussion in the
legislature, reflecting the country's increasing engagement
with the digital economy.

These developments indicate a regional trend towards exploring the
economic opportunities presented by cryptocurrencies, driven by
factors such as high inflation rates, currency devaluation, and
remittance flows.

### 5.3.2. *Caribbean Innovations*

The Caribbean region has been at the forefront of exploring digital
currencies, driven by the need for financial inclusion and efficient
cross-border transactions:

- **The Bahamas** has launched the Sand Dollar, a central bank
  digital currency (CBDC), aiming to enhance financial inclusion
  and reduce transaction costs.

- **Eastern Caribbean Central Bank** (ECCB) has introduced
  DCash, a digital version of the Eastern Caribbean dollar,
  across several member countries, showcasing the region's
  proactive stance on digital finance solutions.

These initiatives reflect the Caribbean's commitment to leveraging
technology to solve economic challenges, potentially inspired by
examples like El Salvador.

### 5.3.3. African and Asian Perspectives

In Africa and Asia, responses to El Salvador's move have been more measured, focusing on regulatory frameworks and the potential of CBDCs:

- **Nigeria**, Africa's largest economy, has launched its own CBDC, the eNaira, aiming to facilitate inclusive financial services and enhance cross-border trade.

- **Despite its cautious stance on cryptocurrencies, India** is exploring the launch of a CBDC while debating the regulatory framework for cryptocurrencies.

- **The Philippines** and **Thailand** have shown interest in developing regulatory frameworks that balance innovation with consumer protection, indicating a keen interest in the potential of digital currencies.

### 5.3.4. European and North American Observations

In Europe and North America, the focus has been more on regulatory clarity and the exploration of CBDCs rather than outright adoption of existing cryptocurrencies like Bitcoin as legal tender:

- **European Union** is working on the Markets in Crypto-Assets (MiCA) regulation to harmonise the approach to cryptocurrencies across member states while exploring a digital euro.

- **The United States** and **Canada** have emphasised regulatory clarity for cryptocurrencies, with discussions around CBDCs gaining momentum among policymakers.

## 6. Taxation and Digital Assets

The rapid ascent of Bitcoin and other digital assets has posed unique challenges for tax authorities worldwide, compelling them to develop frameworks for the taxation of cryptocurrencies. The decentralised nature of digital currencies, coupled with their classification as assets rather than traditional currencies, requires a nuanced approach to taxation that balances innovation with the need to maintain fair tax practices.

### 6.1. Defining Bitcoin for Tax Purposes

#### 6.1.1. Classification Challenges

The classification of Bitcoin for tax purposes is the first hurdle tax authorities face. Unlike fiat currencies issued and regulated by governments, Bitcoin operates on a decentralised network, blurring the lines between currency, commodity, and property. This ambiguity complicates its taxation, as tax treatment can vary significantly based on classification.

#### 6.1.2. Global Perspectives on Classification

- **United States**: The Internal Revenue Service (IRS) classifies cryptocurrencies like Bitcoin as property for tax purposes. Bitcoin transactions are subject to capital gains tax, similar to transactions involving stocks or real estate. The sale, exchange, or use of Bitcoin to purchase goods and services can trigger a taxable event, with the tax rate depending on the length of holding and the taxpayer's income bracket.

- **United Kingdom**: HM Revenue and Customs (HMRC) does not consider cryptocurrencies currency or money. Instead, they are treated as either "chargeable assets" for Capital Gains Tax if held as investments or taxable under Income Tax and National Insurance contributions if received as payment or mining rewards.

- **Australia**: The Australian Taxation Office (ATO) views Bitcoin and other cryptocurrencies as property and an asset for capital gains tax purposes. Like the IRS's approach, cryptocurrency transactions can give rise to capital gains or losses, which must be reported for tax purposes.

- **Germany**: In Germany, Bitcoin is considered private money or a unit of account rather than a currency, commodity, or stock. For individuals, gains are tax-exempt if Bitcoin is held for over a year. It makes Germany one of the more favourable environments for cryptocurrency holders regarding taxation.

### 6.1.3. Taxable Events

Identifying taxable events is crucial for properly taxing Bitcoin and digital assets. Taxable events may include, but are not limited to:

- **Capital Gains**: Realising gains from selling or exchanging Bitcoin for fiat currency, other cryptocurrencies, or purchasing goods and services.

- **Mining and Staking Rewards**: Earnings from mining or staking activities are typically considered taxable income at the time of receipt.

- **Payment for Services**: Receiving Bitcoin in exchange for services is often considered income and subject to income tax.

- **Airdrops and Hard Forks**: Receiving new cryptocurrencies through airdrops or hard forks can constitute a taxable event, with the new assets typically treated as income at their fair market value.

### 6.1.4. *Reporting and Compliance*

For taxpayers, accurately reporting transactions involving Bitcoin and other digital assets can be daunting due to the complexity and novelty of the tax requirements. Tax authorities have started providing guidance and tools to assist in compliance, but the onus remains on the individual to maintain detailed records of their transactions, including dates, values, and the nature of each transaction.

Initially, the term "cryptocurrencies" was predominantly used by regulators to describe the range of digital currencies like Bitcoin, Ethereum, and others that employ cryptographic techniques to secure transactions on decentralised networks. This terminology focused primarily on the currency aspect of these digital assets, emphasising their use as a medium of exchange, a unit of account, and a store of value, akin to traditional fiat currencies but operating within a blockchain framework.

However, as the blockchain and digital asset ecosystem evolved, it became apparent that the innovation and utility of these technologies extended far beyond the conventional functions of money. The emergence of tokens representing a wide variety of assets on blockchain networks, from ownership in real-world assets to digital collectables and access rights to software services, necessitated a broader terminology that could encapsulate the full spectrum of what blockchain technology could represent. It led to the adoption of the term "digital assets" by regulators and industry participants alike.

### 6.1.5.  *From Cryptocurrencies to Digital Assets*

The shift in terminology from "cryptocurrencies" to "digital assets" reflects a recognition of the diverse applications of blockchain technology:

- **Tokenisation of Assets**: Blockchain technology enables the tokenisation of physical and intangible assets, turning them into digital tokens representing ownership or rights over the asset. It can include real estate, art, intellectual property, and more, expanding the scope of what can be traded and owned digitally.

- **Smart Contracts**: Beyond mere currency, blockchain technology facilitates the creation of smart contracts—self-executing contracts with the terms of the agreement directly written into code. This innovation has wide-ranging applications in automating agreements and transactions without intermediaries.

- **Non-Fungible Tokens (NFTs)**: The rise of NFTs showcased the ability of blockchain to create unique, indivisible tokens representing ownership of specific digital or physical assets, particularly in art, gaming, and collectables. NFTs exemplify how digital assets can encapsulate more than just monetary value, including cultural, artistic, and intellectual value.

### 6.1.6. *Regulatory Implications*

The broadening of the regulatory lens to encompass "digital assets" rather than just "cryptocurrencies" signifies an anticipatory move by regulators to address the rapidly evolving landscape of blockchain-based assets. This inclusive terminology allows regulatory frameworks to be more adaptable to new forms of digital assets that may emerge, such as NFTs, without the need for constant revision of legal definitions.

- **Comprehensive Oversight**: By adopting the term "digital assets," regulators aim to ensure comprehensive oversight for the full range of activities and innovations within the digital asset space, including trading, custody, and issuance across various asset classes.

- **Innovation and Protection**: The move seeks to balance promoting innovation and the protection of consumers and investors by providing clarity and legal certainty for entities operating in the digital asset ecosystem.

- **Global Harmonisation**: As digital assets gain global traction, the adoption of common terminology and conceptual frameworks aids in the harmonisation of regulatory approaches, facilitating international cooperation and standard setting.

## 6.2. International Tax Considerations and Challenges

The evolution of the digital asset landscape, including cryptocurrencies like Bitcoin and the emergence of non-fungible tokens (NFTs), has prompted tax authorities worldwide to broaden their terminological and regulatory frameworks. Initially, the term "cryptocurrencies" was predominantly used to describe this new class of assets. However, as the diversity and complexity of these assets grew, regulators expanded their lexicon to "digital assets" to encapsulate a wider range of forms, including cryptocurrencies, utility tokens, security tokens, and NFTs. This shift reflects an effort to anticipate continuous innovation within the sector and address the unique tax considerations and challenges they present internationally.

### 6.2.1.  Broadening the Tax Vocabulary

The transition from "cryptocurrencies" to "digital assets" in regulatory parlance is significant. It acknowledges that the digital asset ecosystem encompasses more than just digital currencies. NFTs, for example, represent a unique type of digital asset that can signify ownership of specific items or rights, differing fundamentally from cryptocurrencies in their non-fungibility. By adopting the broader term, tax authorities and regulatory bodies recognise the evolving nature of digital assets and the need for flexible, comprehensive tax policies that can adapt to future innovations.

### 6.2.2.  International Tax Considerations

As digital assets transcend national borders, they introduce complex international tax considerations:

- **Double Taxation**: The lack of harmonised tax treatment for digital assets can lead to scenarios where different jurisdictions tax the same asset multiple times. International agreements and tax treaties may need updates to address digital assets and explicitly prevent double taxation.

- **Tax Jurisdiction and Residency**: Determining the tax jurisdiction for digital asset transactions can be challenging, especially when these involve parties from multiple countries or are facilitated by decentralised platforms without a clear physical presence. The residency concept for individuals and entities dealing in digital assets becomes crucial in deciding which tax laws apply.

- **Transfer Pricing**: For multinational companies engaging in transactions involving digital assets, transfer pricing becomes a complex issue. The valuation of digital assets, especially unique ones like NFTs, and the allocation of profits and losses across different jurisdictions require clear guidelines to ensure compliance with international tax laws.

### 6.2.3. *Challenges*

The international nature of digital assets poses significant challenges for tax compliance and enforcement:

- **Reporting and Transparency**: A major challenge is Ensuring taxpayers accurately report their digital asset transactions. The pseudonymous nature of many digital transactions complicates the ability of tax authorities to track ownership and gains.

- **Valuation**: The high volatility and market variations of digital assets complicate their valuation for tax purposes. Establishing a consistent approach to valuation across different jurisdictions is necessary for equitable taxation.

- **Regulatory Collaboration**: International collaboration between regulatory bodies is essential to address the global challenges digital assets present. It includes sharing information, standardising regulations, and jointly addressing tax evasion and avoidance schemes involving digital assets.

### 6.3. Compliance and Enforcement

As the digital asset ecosystem continues to expand, compliance and enforcement in the realm of taxation become increasingly paramount. The rapid evolution and adoption of cryptocurrencies, non-fungible tokens (NFTs), and other digital assets have presented unique challenges for tax authorities worldwide. These challenges necessitate robust mechanisms for ensuring compliance with tax laws and regulations and effective strategies for enforcement against evasion and fraud involving digital assets.

#### 6.3.1.  Enhancing Compliance

The first step towards effective taxation of digital assets involves enhancing compliance among taxpayers, which can be achieved through several key strategies:

- **Clear Guidance and Education**: Tax authorities need to provide clear, accessible guidance on the tax obligations related to digital assets. It includes how different types of transactions are taxed, record-keeping requirements, and the process for reporting gains and losses. Educating taxpayers on their responsibilities can significantly increase voluntary compliance.

- **Simplified Reporting Tools**: Developing tools and platforms simplifying calculating and reporting taxes on digital asset transactions can encourage compliance. Integration of these tools with popular cryptocurrency wallets and exchanges can automate much of the reporting process, reducing the burden on taxpayers.

- **Use of Technology for Compliance Verification**: Tax authorities can leverage technology, including blockchain analysis tools, to verify compliance. These tools can trace transactions on the blockchain, identify patterns indicative of tax evasion, and help tax authorities understand the flow of digital assets.

### 6.3.2. Strategies for Enforcement

Despite efforts to enhance compliance, enforcement actions are necessary to address tax evasion and fraud involving digital assets. Effective enforcement strategies may include:

- **Collaboration with Exchanges and Wallet Providers**: Tax authorities can work with cryptocurrency exchanges, wallet providers, and other intermediaries to obtain transaction data for tax enforcement purposes. It requires a legal framework that mandates reporting by these entities, similar to traditional financial institutions.

- **International Cooperation**: Given the global nature of the digital asset market, international cooperation is crucial for enforcement. Sharing information and collaborating on investigations can help tax authorities track cross-border transactions and tackle tax evasion schemes that span multiple jurisdictions.

- **Legal and Regulatory Framework**: Strengthening the legal and regulatory framework surrounding digital assets is essential for effective enforcement. It includes defining the powers of tax authorities to investigate and prosecute tax evasion involving digital assets and establishing penalties that deter non-compliance.

- **Public Awareness Campaigns**: Raising public awareness about the legal consequences of evading taxes on digital asset transactions can deter non-compliance. Highlighting successful enforcement actions can reinforce the message that tax authorities are equipped to identify and prosecute tax evasion in the digital asset space.

### 6.3.3.  *Challenges in Compliance and Enforcement*

The decentralised and pseudonymous nature of many digital asset transactions poses significant challenges for compliance and enforcement. Addressing these challenges requires ongoing adaptation of tax laws and regulations and continuous investment in technology and international collaboration. Additionally, striking the right balance between encouraging innovation in the digital asset sector and ensuring fair taxation will remain a key concern for policymakers.

## 7.  Bitcoin vs Central Bank Digital Currencies (CBDCs)

The financial landscape is witnessing the emergence of two significant digital currency models: decentralised cryptocurrencies, with Bitcoin at the forefront, and Central Bank Digital Currencies (CBDCs), digital forms of a country's fiat currency issued and regulated by its central bank. While both aim to capitalise on digital technology to improve financial transactions, their underlying philosophies, objectives, and mechanisms differ.

### 7.1. Understanding CBDCs: Objectives and Mechanisms

*7.1.1.  Objectives of CBDCs*

- **Financial Inclusion**: One of the primary objectives of CBDCs is to enhance financial inclusion by providing an accessible and efficient means of payment and store of value, especially for unbanked and underbanked populations.

- **Efficiency and Lower Costs**: CBDCs aim to make financial transactions more efficient and less expensive by reducing the reliance on physical cash and streamlining payment systems, potentially lowering transaction fees and processing times.

- **Economic Policy Implementation**: By issuing digital currencies, central banks gain a new tool for implementing monetary policy more effectively. For instance, CBDCs could enable more direct mechanisms for adjusting interest rates or distributing stimulus payments.

- **Stability and Security**: CBDCs offer a secure and stable digital currency backed by the central bank, providing a safer alternative to private digital currencies and ensuring the currency's value is not subject to the same volatility in cryptocurrencies like Bitcoin.

### 7.1.2. Mechanisms of CBDCs

- **Centralised Issuance and Control**: Unlike cryptocurrencies, which operate on decentralised networks, CBDCs are issued and controlled by a central authority, the country's central bank. This centralisation ensures the digital currency remains tied to the country's monetary policy and financial regulatory framework.

- **Two-Tier System**: Most CBDC models propose a two-tier system where the central bank issues the digital currency, but commercial banks and other financial institutions handle the distribution and retail operations. This approach leverages existing banking infrastructure while introducing digital currency into the economy.

- **Technology Platforms**: While some CBDC projects explore blockchain or distributed ledger technology (DLT) for their underlying infrastructure, others may opt for more centralised digital ledger solutions. The choice of technology impacts the CBDC's scalability, security, and interoperability with existing financial systems.

- **Privacy and Compliance**: CBDCs are designed to balance user privacy with regulatory compliance, including anti-money laundering (AML) and counter-terrorism financing (CTF) measures. Unlike the pseudonymous nature of transactions in cryptocurrencies like Bitcoin, CBDC transactions may be subject to identity verification processes to meet regulatory standards.

### 7.1.3. Comparison with Bitcoin

The contrast between Bitcoin and CBDCs lies not only in their technological mechanisms but also in their foundational principles. Bitcoin's decentralised, permissionless nature challenges the traditional financial system, offering a form of money that is not controlled by any single entity and is censorship-resistant. In contrast, CBDCs reinforce the existing financial system, providing a digital currency that retains the characteristics of fiat money, including central control and regulation.

## 7.2. The Key Differences: Decentralisation, Privacy, and Control

The distinctions between Bitcoin and Central Bank Digital Currencies (CBDCs) in terms of decentralisation, privacy, and control encapsulate the evolving debate on the future of money and its role in society. These differences are not merely technical; they represent a broader philosophical and ideological debate about the nature of financial sovereignty, privacy rights, and the balance of power between individuals and the state.

### 7.2.1. Philosophical Underpinnings

- **Bitcoin** emerges from a libertarian and cypherpunk ethos that values financial sovereignty, privacy, and resistance to centralised control. Its decentralised nature challenges traditional financial models, proposing an alternative where trust is placed in code and community consensus rather than central banks or governments.

- **CBDCs** represent state institutions attempting to harness the efficiencies and innovations of digital currency technology while maintaining control over monetary policy and financial regulation. They reflect a continuity of the state's role in issuing and managing currency, updated for the digital age.

### 7.2.2. *Implications for Users and the Financial System*

- **User Autonomy vs. Oversight**: Bitcoin gives users a high degree of autonomy, allowing them to transact without oversight or permission from authorities. In contrast, CBDCs, with their centralised control, could enable greater surveillance and oversight of financial transactions, raising concerns about privacy and financial freedom.

- **Innovation and Stability**: Bitcoin's decentralised model fosters innovation and offers a censorship-resistant form of money but comes with challenges related to volatility and scalability. CBDCs, while potentially less innovative in decentralisation, promise greater stability and could be designed to scale efficiently within the existing financial infrastructure.

- **Financial Inclusion**: Bitcoin and CBDCs can potentially advance financial inclusion. Bitcoin can provide financial services to those without access to traditional banking, while

CBDCs, backed by central banks, could be specifically designed to serve underserved communities.

### 7.2.3.  The Broader Economics

The coexistence of Bitcoin, CBDCs, and traditional fiat currencies paints a complex picture of the future economic landscape, where different forms of money cater to varied needs, preferences, and philosophical orientations. This diversity could lead to a more resilient and inclusive financial system but necessitates careful application of interoperability, privacy, and regulatory compliance issues.

### 7.3. The Future Context of Digital Currencies

The decision to focus exclusively on Bitcoin, rather than incorporating a broader spectrum of cryptocurrencies, is grounded in several key considerations related to Bitcoin's unique position in the digital currency landscape, its pioneering role, and the specific functions it has come to embody.

#### 7.3.1. Pioneering Status

**First Cryptocurrency**: As the first cryptocurrency, Bitcoin introduced the concept of decentralised digital currency to the world. Its launch in 2009 marked the beginning of the cryptocurrency era, setting the foundation for the subsequent development of thousands of other digital currencies. Focusing on Bitcoin allows us to explore cryptocurrency's genesis and understand the core principles that have inspired an entire industry.

#### 7.3.2. Market Dominance

**Largest Market Capitalisation**: Bitcoin remains the cryptocurrency with the largest market capitalisation, representing a significant portion of the total value of the cryptocurrency market. This dominance makes it a focal point for investors, regulators, and the media and positions it as a primary subject of study for anyone seeking to understand cryptocurrencies' economic, technological, and societal impacts.

#### 7.3.3. Infrastructure and Adoption

**Widest Adoption**: Bitcoin has achieved the widest adoption among cryptocurrencies in terms of user base and infrastructure. It is supported by the most extensive network of exchanges, wallets, and payment services, making it the most accessible and usable cryptocurrency for the general public. This widespread adoption provides a rich context for discussing the challenges and opportunities of integrating digital currencies into the global financial system.

### 7.3.4. Symbolic and Cultural Significance

**Cultural Impact**: Beyond its technical and financial aspects, Bitcoin has become a cultural phenomenon, symbolising the potential for a new financial system that is more inclusive, transparent, and resistant to censorship. It represents a shift in thinking about money, sovereignty, and the power structures within the global economy. Focusing on Bitcoin allows for exploring these broader cultural and ideological shifts.

### 7.3.5. Regulatory and Policy Focus

**Regulatory Attention**: Bitcoin has been the primary focus of regulatory bodies and policymakers as they face the challenges and opportunities presented by cryptocurrencies. Studying Bitcoin's interactions with regulatory frameworks worldwide offers insights into the evolving landscape of digital currency regulation and its implications for privacy, security, and financial autonomy.

### 7.3.6. Technical Foundation and Innovations

**Technological Innovations**: Bitcoin introduced the blockchain, a groundbreaking technology with applications far beyond cryptocurrencies. By examining Bitcoin, the book can delve into the technical underpinnings of blockchain technology, its potential uses, and its challenges regarding scalability, energy consumption, and security.

## 8.   Conclusions and Reflections

### 8.1. Assessing Bitcoin's Impact on Finance and Society

Bitcoin's emergence and decade-long journey have undeniably profoundly impacted finance, technology, and society. Its impact extends beyond the realms of currency and investment, challenging traditional notions of money, the role of central authorities in financial transactions, and the potential for decentralised technologies. This section reflects on the multifaceted impact of Bitcoin.

#### 8.1.1.   *Transformation of the Financial Sector*

- **Decentralisation of Finance**: Bitcoin introduced the concept of decentralised finance (DeFi), demonstrating that financial transactions can occur directly between parties without traditional intermediaries like banks. It has inspired a whole ecosystem of DeFi applications, promising more accessible, efficient, and transparent financial services.

- **Innovation in Payment Systems**: Bitcoin has shown the feasibility of instant, cross-border payments with lower fees than traditional banking systems. It has pressured financial institutions to innovate and improve their payment systems to remain competitive.

- **Rise of Cryptocurrency Markets**: The success of Bitcoin paved the way for thousands of other cryptocurrencies, each with unique features and purposes. The cryptocurrency market has become a significant part of the global financial landscape, offering new investment opportunities and challenges.

### 8.1.2. Societal Impact

- **Financial Inclusion**: Bitcoin can increase financial inclusion by providing access to financial services for unbanked and underbanked populations. Its ability to facilitate transactions without the need for a traditional banking infrastructure offers a pathway to economic participation for millions.

- **Awareness and Discussion about Money and Privacy**: Bitcoin has spurred widespread discussion about the nature of money, privacy, and the state's role in regulating currency and finance. It has raised awareness about financial surveillance and the importance of privacy in financial transactions, contributing to a broader debate about digital rights and freedoms.

- **Inspiration for Blockchain Applications**: Beyond finance, Bitcoin's underlying blockchain technology has inspired applications across various sectors, including supply chain management, healthcare, and governance. These applications promise to enhance transparency, security, and efficiency in processes and record-keeping.

### 8.1.3. Challenges and Controversies

- **Regulatory and Legal Issues**: Bitcoin's growth has been accompanied by regulatory challenges as governments and financial authorities grapple with integrating it within existing legal and regulatory frameworks. Taxation, anti-money laundering (AML) efforts, and consumer protection remain significant challenges.

- **Environmental Concerns**: The energy consumption associated with Bitcoin mining has raised environmental concerns, highlighting the need for sustainable practices within the cryptocurrency sector. It has spurred efforts to find more energy-efficient consensus mechanisms and to increase the use of renewable energy sources in mining operations.

- **Volatility and Speculation**: The high volatility of Bitcoin and other cryptocurrencies has led to debates about their viability as a store of value and medium of exchange. While some view the volatility as a sign of speculative bubbles, others see it as a natural aspect of a new and evolving market.

## 8.2. The Ongoing Debate: Innovation vs Regulation

An ongoing debate between the forces of innovation and the needs for regulation marks the trajectory of Bitcoin and the broader cryptocurrency landscape. This debate encapsulates the tension between fostering technological advancements and ensuring financial stability, consumer protection, and compliance with laws designed to prevent financial crimes. Both innovation and regulation are crucial for the sustainable development of the cryptocurrency ecosystem, but finding the right balance between them remains a complex challenge.

### 8.2.1.  The Case for Innovation

- **Technological Breakthroughs**: Bitcoin and blockchain technology represent significant innovations in digital finance, offering new ways of conducting transactions, securing data, and building decentralised applications. These innovations have the potential to enhance efficiency, reduce costs, and create new economic opportunities.

- **Financial Inclusion**: Cryptocurrencies offer a path to financial inclusion for the unbanked and underbanked populations by providing access to financial services without the need for traditional banking infrastructure.

- **Empowerment and Autonomy**: By enabling peer-to-peer transactions without central intermediaries, cryptocurrencies empower individuals, giving them more control over their financial transactions and reducing their dependence on traditional financial institutions.

### 8.2.2.  *The Need for Regulation*

- **Consumer Protection**: Regulation is essential to protect consumers from fraud, scams, and cryptocurrency volatility. Clear regulatory frameworks can help build trust in the ecosystem, making it safer for individuals and businesses to adopt and use digital currencies.

- **Financial Stability**: The integration of cryptocurrencies into the global financial system raises concerns about potential impacts on financial stability. Regulators aim to ensure that the rise of digital currencies does not introduce systemic risks that could affect broader economic health.

- **Preventing Illicit Activities**: Cryptocurrencies have been used for illicit activities, including money laundering, terrorism financing, and tax evasion. Regulation is necessary to prevent misuse while maintaining privacy and security.

### 8.2.3.  *Finding a Balance*

The challenge lies in implementing regulatory frameworks that do not stifle innovation. Regulation should aim to support the positive aspects of cryptocurrencies while addressing potential risks. It requires a nuanced approach that evolves alongside technological advancements and market developments. Key considerations include:

- **Adaptive Regulation**: Regulatory frameworks should be flexible enough to adapt to new technological developments and innovative use cases within the cryptocurrency space.

- **International Collaboration**: Given the global nature of cryptocurrencies, international collaboration among regulatory bodies is crucial to creating consistent and effective regulations.

- **Stakeholder Engagement**: Regulators should engage with a broad range of stakeholders, including technologists, entrepreneurs, and consumer advocacy groups, to understand the implications of proposed regulations and ensure they support healthy innovation.

- **Clear and Consistent Guidelines**: Providing clear, consistent guidelines can help reduce uncertainty for businesses operating in the cryptocurrency space, encouraging responsible innovation and investment.

### 8.3. Looking Ahead: What the Future Holds for Bitcoin and Digital Currencies

As we stand at the crossroads of the digital currency revolution, the future of Bitcoin and digital currencies is a subject of intense speculation and interest. Several factors will shape the trajectory of Bitcoin and its peers, influencing the cryptocurrency market and the broader financial, technological, and social landscapes. While predicting the future with certainty is impossible, several trends and developments offer insights into what may lie ahead.

#### 8.3.1. Integration into Mainstream Finance

- **Institutional Adoption**: Increasing interest from institutional investors, financial services, and corporations suggests a growing integration of Bitcoin and digital currencies into mainstream finance. This trend will likely continue, leading to more stable markets and broader acceptance as legitimate financial instruments.

- **Payment Systems and Retail**: Advances in payment technology and growing merchant acceptance are making it easier to use Bitcoin and other digital currencies for everyday transactions. Over time, this could enhance the usability of cryptocurrencies, moving them closer to becoming viable alternatives to traditional money for a wider audience.

#### 8.3.2. Technological Innovations

- **Layer 2 and Beyond**: Technologies like the Lightning Network (for Bitcoin) and other layer 2 solutions address scalability and transaction speed issues, making digital currencies more practical for everyday use. Continued innovation in this space is crucial for overcoming current limitations and unlocking new possibilities for cryptocurrency applications.

- **Interoperability**: Efforts to enhance interoperability between blockchain networks will be key to a cohesive digital currency ecosystem. It could lead to more seamless exchanges of value across platforms and further integration of various digital assets into a unified financial system.

### 8.3.3. Regulatory Landscapes

- **Global Regulation**: The regulatory environment for cryptocurrencies is expected to evolve, with more countries establishing clear frameworks for digital assets. Effective regulation that protects consumers while supporting innovation could significantly influence the adoption and development of digital currencies.

- **Privacy vs. Compliance**: Balancing the privacy features of digital currencies with regulatory compliance requirements (AML, CTF, KYC) will remain a contentious issue. Innovations that preserve user privacy while ensuring transparency for regulatory purposes will be critical in managing this balance.

### 8.3.4. Societal and Economic Impact

- **Financial Inclusion**: Digital currencies promise to enhance financial inclusion globally, especially in underserved regions. Continued efforts to make digital assets accessible and usable for unbanked populations could have profound social and economic impacts.

- **Decentralised Finance (DeFi)**: The rise of DeFi platforms demonstrates the potential for a financial system that operates independently of traditional banking and financial institutions. The growth and maturation of DeFi could redefine lending, borrowing, and investing in the digital age.

- **Central Bank Digital Currencies (CBDCs)**: The development and rollout of CBDCs will likely coexist with cryptocurrencies like Bitcoin, offering a digital alternative backed by central banks. The interaction between CBDCs and decentralised cryptocurrencies will be a fascinating area to watch, potentially influencing monetary policy, payment systems, and the role of central banks.